THE WEALTH HACK

7 Simple Shifts to Go from Broke to Financially Free

C.C. Gayle

"The secret to wealth is simple: Find a way to do more for others than anyone else does."

— Tony Robbins

Copyright

The Wealth Hack:
7 Simple Shifts to Go from Broke to Financially Free
Copyright © 2025 by C.C. Gayle
All rights reserved.

No part of this publication may be reproduced, stored in a retrieval system, or transmitted in any form or by any means—electronic, mechanical, photocopying, recording, or otherwise—without prior written permission of the author or publisher, except for brief quotations used in reviews or scholarly articles.

This book is independently published and is not affiliated with any financial institution or advisory service.

Disclaimer: This book is for informational and educational purposes only. The author and publisher are not financial advisors, and nothing contained herein should be considered professional financial advice. Readers are encouraged to consult a qualified advisor before making any financial decisions.

Published by Elevate Ink Publishing
Printed in the United States of America
First Edition: April 2025
ISBN: 979-8-9986666-1-2

Dedication

"To those who refuse to accept financial struggle as their destiny—

this book is for you."

Preface

For years, I struggled financially, thinking the key to wealth was just 'working harder.' But after studying self-made millionaires, I realized that success starts with mental shifts. This book distills those shifts into 7 actionable steps that changed my life—and can change yours too.

Table of Contents

Introduction: The Science of Financial Transformation 06

Chapter 1: The Millionaire Mindset Shift 12

Chapter 2: The High-Income Skill Shift 21

Chapter 3: The Ownership Shift 31

Chapter 4: The Automation Shift 41

Chapter 5: The Frictionless Income Shift 51

Chapter 6: The Network Shift 61

Chapter 7: The Legacy Shift 71

Conclusion: Your 7-Shift Game Plan 81

Bonus 1: Wealth Tracking & Goal-Setting Workbook 92

Bonus 2: Resources & Recommended Reading List 98

Acknowledgements 103

Introduction

The Science of Financial Transformation

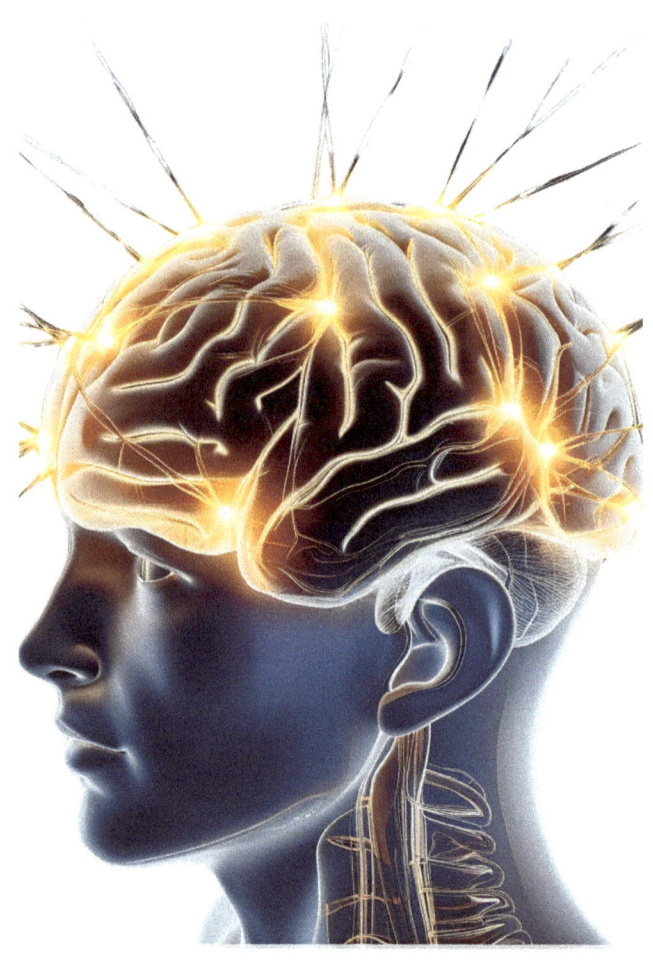

Introduction:
The Science of Financial Transformation

Why Do Most People Struggle Financially?

If you're reading this book, chances are you're looking for a way to break free from financial stress and finally take control of your money. Maybe you feel like you work hard but never get ahead. Maybe you've tried budgeting, saving, or investing, yet it always feels like there's never enough left over.

You're not alone.

Most people struggle financially—not because they're lazy, and not because they don't want success—perhaps because they've been programmed with **the wrong financial beliefs** from an early age.

Think about it.

From childhood, we're taught:
- "Money doesn't grow on trees."
- "You have to work hard for money."
- "Rich people are lucky or greedy."
- "Just go to school, get a job, and you'll be fine."

Society trains us to be **good employees, not wealth builders.** We're taught how to trade time for money but never how to make money work for us.

And that's the first problem—**most people approach money with a broken mindset.**

Here's the good news: You **can** reprogram your mind for wealth. And it all starts with shifting how you think about money.

The Power of Mental Shifts Over Just Financial Tactics

You might think financial success is about learning strategies—budgeting, saving, investing, or making more money. And while those are important, here's the truth:

Your financial success isn't determined by how much money you make—it's determined by how you think about money.

Consider this:

- **Two people** can earn the same amount, yet one struggles while the other builds wealth.
- **Lottery winners** often lose their fortunes within years because they never shifted their mindset.
- **Self-made millionaires** build their fortunes not just through tactics, but through mindset shifts.

Your mindset is the foundation of your wealth. Without the right mindset, no amount of money will ever be enough. With the right mindset, even small amounts of money can be turned into financial freedom.

This book isn't about just teaching financial strategies—it's about **rewiring how you think about wealth so you can attract and keep more money.**

How Self-Made Millionaires Think Differently About Money

The truth is, **millionaires don't think about money the way most people do.**

Here's how they see things differently:

- **They focus on assets, not income.** While most people focus on earning a paycheck, millionaires focus on buying and building assets that generate money for them.
- **They don't trade time for money.** Instead of relying on a single paycheck, they create multiple income streams and passive income sources.
- **They view money as a tool, not a goal.** While most people chase money, millionaires see it as a resource to create freedom, opportunities, and impact.
- **They surround themselves with success.** They know that wealth is contagious—so they spend time with people who encourage and push them toward higher aspirations.
- **They think long-term.** Most people focus on immediate financial struggles, but millionaires plan for **years and decades ahead.**

The good news? **You don't have to be born into wealth to start thinking like the wealthy.** You can adopt these principles **today.**

The 7 Shifts That Will Change Your Financial Life

The reason most financial advice doesn't work is that it **only focuses on tactics**—budgeting, investing, saving—without addressing the mental blocks that keep people stuck.

That's why this book is different.

Instead of just teaching you **what** to do, we're going to focus on **how to think and act like a self-made millionaire.**

Inside, you'll discover **7 powerful mindset and financial shifts** that will help you go from broke to financially free:

Shift #1: The Millionaire Mindset Shift
- How to reprogram your beliefs about money and success.

Shift #2: The High-Income Skill Shift
- Why trading time for money keeps you stuck and how to develop high-income skills.

Shift #3: The Ownership Shift
- How to stop being a consumer and start being an investor.

Shift #4: The Automation Shift
- How to make money work for you instead of the other way around.

Shift #5: The Frictionless Income Shift
- How to create multiple income streams so you're never dependent on one paycheck.

Shift #6: The Network Shift
- How to surround yourself with the right people who will elevate your success.

Shift #7: The Legacy Shift
- How to build wealth that lasts beyond your lifetime.

These 7 shifts are **proven, science-backed, and used by self-made millionaires worldwide.** If you're ready to transform your financial life, let's dive in.

Key References:

- *The Psychology of Money* – Understanding the emotional side of money.
- *Rich Dad Poor Dad* – How beliefs about money shape financial outcomes.

Chapter 1

The Millionaire Mindset Shift

Reprogramming Your Money Beliefs

At 27, **Lisa** was drowning in debt, earning just enough to survive. She grew up hearing, "Money doesn't grow on trees," and believed wealth was for the lucky or privileged. Then she met **Mia**, a former barista who became a millionaire in five years. Mia told her, "Wealth isn't about luck—it's about mindset." Intrigued, Lisa started studying how self-made millionaires thought differently. Instead of saying, "I can't afford it," she asked, "How can I create value to afford it?" That shift changed everything.

Chapter 1: The Millionaire Mindset Shift Reprogramming Your Money Beliefs

Introduction to the Millionaire Mindset

The first step in transforming your financial life is to reprogram your mindset.

You see, **wealth is not just about earning money**—it's about changing the way you think about it. And the way you think about money is deeply rooted in your **beliefs and psychology.**

Most people struggle with money because of **limiting beliefs** that they've unconsciously adopted over the years. These beliefs are often passed down from family, society, or media and are deeply ingrained in our subconscious.

Think about this:
- Do you believe that wealth is for "other people"?
- Have you been taught that money is "hard to come by"?
- Do you often feel like there's never enough to go around?

If you answered "yes" to any of these, it's time to **reprogram** your beliefs. Self-made millionaires don't think like this. They understand that **money is abundant,** and they have the right mindset to attract it.

In this chapter, you'll discover how to **break free from your limiting beliefs** and adopt a millionaire mindset that will set you on the path to financial freedom.

The Neuroscience of Financial Decisions

To understand how to shift your mindset, we need to first understand **how your brain works when it comes to money.**

When you think about money, your brain doesn't just process numbers. It also triggers deep-seated **emotions**—fear, guilt, shame, or even excitement and pleasure.

Your brain's **limbic system**, the emotional center, is activated when you think about your finances. And over time, this system associates money with specific **emotions** and **beliefs**.

The brain also loves **habit**—so, if you've been stuck in a certain financial pattern, like scarcity or financial anxiety, your brain has developed a **habit** of thinking that way. But don't worry, the brain is incredibly adaptable!

Through consistent practice and perseverance, you can reprogram the brain and develop new habits in line with financial abundance. And the first step is realizing that **your current beliefs about money are not set in stone.**

Breaking Free from the Scarcity Mindset

One of the biggest obstacles to wealth is the **scarcity mindset**—the belief that there's never enough.

This mindset is often shaped by the way we're raised, societal pressures, or past financial struggles. People with a scarcity mindset believe:
- "I have to work harder to get more money."
- "There's never enough to go around."
- "Rich people are selfish or greedy."

This belief leads to behaviors like **overworking, undersaving,** and **fearing investments**—because you're constantly worried that there won't be enough money to go around.

The key to financial independence is shifting from a mentality of scarcity to one of abundance.

An **abundance mindset** allows you to see opportunities rather than limitations. It's the belief that **money is plentiful** and that your efforts will be rewarded. It's understanding that wealth is a means for freedom, impact, and growth, not a finite resource.

Adopting an Abundance Mindset

To shift from scarcity to abundance, start by **challenging your old beliefs.**

Ask yourself:

- **What beliefs about money was I taught growing up?**
- **Are those beliefs limiting me today?**
- **What new beliefs can I adopt that will serve my financial growth?**

For example, instead of thinking, "There's never enough money," you could reframe it as, "Money is abundant, and I am capable of attracting it in many ways."

Practical Exercise: Mindset Shifting

- **Write down 3 money beliefs** you've held onto in the past.
- **Rewrite them** with an abundance-focused mindset.
- Repeat these new beliefs to yourself daily, and begin noticing how your actions and thoughts shift.

By doing this every day, you'll begin to rewire your brain and become aware of new opportunities for wealth.

The Identity Shift – Seeing Yourself as a Future Wealthy Person

Now that you've started to shift your mindset, it's time to **change the way you see yourself.**

Identity is powerful. How you see yourself influences what you're willing to achieve, how much money you're willing to attract, and even how you handle setbacks.

Self-made millionaires don't just **think about** wealth—they **identify** as wealthy people. They believe in themselves as being able, competent, and deserving of success.

Ask yourself:
- How do I currently identify myself financially?
- Do I see myself as someone who can create wealth?
- How do I see other wealthy people, and how can I relate to them?

It's time to make the **identity shift**. See yourself as a future wealthy person who makes empowered financial decisions, attracts abundance, and takes ownership of their financial future.

Embracing the Wealthy Identity

To fully embrace this new identity, take action aligned with who you want to become. Millionaires don't just think they're wealthy—they **act** wealthy, even before they reach their financial goals.

Here's how you can begin:

- **Take responsibility** for your financial future—stop blaming external circumstances or past mistakes.
- **Invest in yourself**—read books, attend seminars, or seek out mentors who have what you want.
- **Start making money work for you**—whether it's through savings, investments, or starting a side hustle.

By taking on the wealthy identity, you'll begin to attract wealth, opportunity, and success in ways you never thought possible.

Practical Wealth Tactics: Reprogramming Your Money Beliefs

Now that you understand the power of mindset in wealth-building, here's how to take action **right now:**

1 Track Your Money Stories
- Write down your earliest memories about money. What were you told about wealth? What do you feel as a result of these stories?
- Identify any limiting beliefs (e.g., "Money is hard to earn," "Rich people are greedy").

2 Challenge and Replace Limiting Beliefs
- For every negative belief, write a counterstatement (e.g., "Money is a tool for freedom," "Wealth allows me to help others").
- Repeat these affirmations daily to rewire your subconscious mind.

3 Adopt an Abundance Ritual
- Start your mornings by **visualizing your financial freedom**—see yourself achieving your goals.
- Keep a gratitude journal focusing on financial wins (no matter how small).

4 Surround Yourself with Abundance Thinkers
- Follow wealth-positive influencers and authors.
- Engage in communities where financial growth is discussed **in an empowering way.**

Key Takeaways

- Your mindset is the foundation of wealth-building. **Mindset matters more than tactics**—the way you think about money shapes your financial success.

- Break free from the **scarcity mindset** and adopt an **abundance mindset** that sees money as a tool for freedom and growth. Daily habits like visualization and gratitude train your brain for abundance.

- Identify and replace limiting beliefs about money. **Reprogram your beliefs** about money and practice shifting your thoughts to support financial growth.

- Surrounding yourself with the right influences accelerates your success. Embrace the **identity of a future wealthy person,** and start making decisions that align with your financial goals.

By the end of this chapter, you will begin to feel a shift in how you perceive money. Remember, it's not about **how much you have now**—it's about your mindset and the choices you make today to build your future wealth.

Reflection Exercise

What's one limiting belief about money you've held for years? How can you shift it today?

Chapter 2

The High-Income Skill Shift

Stop Trading Time for Money

- Start Trading Value

James drove for Uber full-time, barely making ends meet. One day, a wealthy businessman he picked up told him, "You're not stuck—you're just lacking the right skill." That advice haunted James. He started researching high-income skills and taught himself **copywriting** through free online resources. Within a year, he landed freelance gigs, quit Uber, and within three years, was making six figures working remotely. Skills, not salaries, build wealth.

Chapter 2: The High-Income Skill Shift
Stop Trading Time for Money – Start Trading Value

Introduction to High-Income Skills

In the modern economy, **time is the most valuable asset**—but it's also the one thing you can never get back. Most people trade their time for money, exchanging hours worked for a fixed paycheck. But this trade, while necessary, limits your potential and financial growth.

Self-made millionaires **don't trade time for money.** Instead, they leverage their skills and knowledge to **create value.** They understand that **high-income skills** allow them to earn exponentially more while working smarter, not harder.

What's a high-income skill?

A high-income skill is any skill that enables you to generate a large amount of money by providing value that others are willing to pay for. Unlike traditional jobs, where your earning potential is capped by your hourly rate, high-income skills allow you to control your income by providing services or creating products that solve big problems.

In this chapter, you'll discover the **importance of high-income skills** and how they can change your financial future. But first, let's break down why learning and mastering these skills is your key to financial freedom.

The Trap of the 9-to-5 Mentality

The traditional "9-to-5" job was designed during a time when most people were focused on surviving rather than thriving. If you're still stuck in the **9-to-5 trap**, you're likely trading **time for money**. This type of system holds you back from making as much money as you can and locks you into the trap of more hours for more money, yet never actually progressing.

It's a cycle that only leads to **burnout** and **financial frustration**. Most people have been conditioned to think that the only way to increase income is by working longer hours, but **self-made millionaires think differently.** They realize that there is a smarter way to build wealth.

The key to breaking free from the trap is to earn more money through acquiring skills such that you don't necessarily need to work longer hours.

What are High-Income Skills?

High-income skills are **specific, marketable abilities** that can command a premium salary or fee in the marketplace. They require specialized skills or expertise, and they resolve a problem or fill a need that someone else will pay for.

Here are a few examples of **high-income skills:**
- Sales
- Copywriting
- Digital Marketing
- Consulting
- Public Speaking
- Software Development
- Graphic Design
- Negotiation

These skills are in high demand and can be used in almost any industry. **The common denominator** between all high-income skills is that they enable you to **create value** for others in a way that justifies a premium price.

The beauty of high-income skills is that they **don't rely on an employer** to pay you a set salary. You can be a freelancer, consultant, or entrepreneur, giving you control over your earning potential.

Why High-Income Skills Matter

Let's take a deeper look at why **high-income skills** are so powerful. If you want to go from **broke to financially free**, you must start thinking in terms of **value creation**.

The most successful people in the world aren't focused on their hourly rate; they're focused on **creating value** at scale. When you learn a high-income skill, you're able to charge more money for your expertise and create wealth without having to work more hours.

But here's the catch: It's not just about **mastering a skill**—it's about **becoming known for that skill.** You can be the best copywriter in the world, but if nobody knows who you are, you won't command top-dollar for your work. Your goal is to **combine skill mastery with personal branding**, so you can charge premium prices for your expertise.

The "Skill-Stacking" Strategy

One of the **most powerful strategies** for increasing your earning potential is **skill-stacking**.

Skill stacking is the concept of **combining multiple complementary skills** to create a unique value proposition that sets you apart from the competition. For example, imagine you're a **digital marketer** with a background in **psychology**. You can combine these two skills and specialize in consumer behavior, and you will be a very much in-demand asset to companies.

The goal is to stack **high-demand skills** that complement one another, allowing you to increase your earning potential dramatically. The more unique and valuable your skill set is, the more you can charge.

For instance, a **copywriter** who also has **knowledge of SEO, social media marketing**, and **data analytics** is in far more demand than a basic copywriter. This combination of skills will allow you to command higher prices for jobs and clients.

How to Identify Your High-Income Skills

You may be wondering: "How do I identify which high-income skill to develop?" It's simple: Look at where your **interests and strengths overlap with market demand.**

Step 1: Identify Your Interests
What do you love to do? What areas are you most compelled? The more interested you are in a subject, you're more likely to stick with it and do well.

Step 2: Evaluate Market Demand
Which skills are in high demand in the marketplace? What does everyone require? Look at high-income professions using websites such as LinkedIn, Upwork, and job postings, and figure out what employers and customers need.

Step 3: Find the Intersection
Now, find where your passions and the market demand intersect. If you love writing and have a knack for persuasion, **copywriting** could be your high-income skill. If you love technology and data, **software development** might be a fit.

Mastering the High-Income Skill

The key to unlocking your financial freedom is **mastering your high-income skill.**

You don't have to be perfect, but you do need to **practice consistently.** The more you practice, the better you become, and the more you can charge for your services. Put it this way: The more skillful you become at something, the more **value** you can deliver to others. And **value is directly tied to income.**

Start by dedicating time each day to improving your high-income skill. Whether it's taking online courses, reading books, or getting hands-on experience, every little bit of progress you make will increase your value in the marketplace.

Practical Wealth Tactics: Mastering High-Income Skills

Now that you understand the importance of high-income skills, take these **concrete steps** to develop yours:

1 Identify Your Core Strengths
- Write down what people ask you for advice on.
- Consider skills in sales, marketing, coding, consulting, or writing—high-income skills.

2 Commit to Learning a New High-Income Skill
- Take an online course or read books from industry leaders.
- Dedicate at least 30 minutes a day to practicing or learning your chosen skill.

3 Monetize Your Skills
- Offer freelance work on platforms like Upwork or Fiverr.
- Create a portfolio showcasing your skills and expertise.

4 Scale Your Skills
- Network with industry experts.
- Find ways to automate or delegate work to increase your earning potential.

Key Takeaways

- **High-income skills** are the key to earning more money while working less. Gaining high-income skills allows you the opportunity to have financial freedom, to call your own shots, and create wealth on your own terms.

- **Start by identifying your strengths** and committing to learning. Find your passion and strengths, and determine a high-income skill that is in demand in the market.

- Once you **master your skills** through consistent practice, you will become known as the expert. Instead of trading time for money, focus on **creating value** that can scale. Monetize your skills through freelancing or business opportunities.

- **Skill stacking is a powerful strategy** for increasing your earning potential. Scaling and automation increase long-term profitability.

By the end of this chapter, you should have a clear understanding of why **high-income skills** are vital for financial freedom and how you can begin mastering one today.

Reflection Exercise

Which high-income skill do you want to master, and how will you take your first step today?

Chapter 3

The Ownership Shift

From Consumer to Investor

Eric and **Mark** both made $50K a year. Eric bought a new car, leased an expensive apartment, and lived paycheck to paycheck. Mark, however, lived modestly and invested in stocks and rental properties. Fast forward ten years: Eric was still stuck in the rat race, while Mark had multiple income streams and financial freedom. What was their difference? Mark prioritized **ownership over consumption.**

Chapter 3: The Ownership Shift

From Consumer to Investor

Introduction to the Ownership Shift

The **ownership shift** is one of the most profound changes in the way people approach wealth. Most individuals are consumers. They spend money on goods, services, and experiences, often without realizing that **owning assets**—whether they are real estate, stocks, or even a business—is the true path to **financial freedom.**

Self-made millionaires aren't just consumers; they are **investors**. They understand that **building wealth requires acquiring assets** that generate income over time, rather than merely spending money on things that depreciate in value.

In this chapter, we will break down the shift from being a **consumer to an investor**—and why it is essential if you want to escape the cycle of financial struggle and move towards **financial independence.**

The Problem with Consumerism

From an early age, society teaches us to be **consumers**. We are encouraged to buy the latest gadgets, fashionable clothes, and expensive cars. The culture of consumerism is so ingrained in our daily lives that it feels like the natural way of living. **Advertisers, media, and peers** bombard us with messages that equate **spending with success.**

But here's the harsh truth: **Consumerism keeps you poor.**

Every time you buy something that doesn't appreciate in value—like a car, a brand-new phone, or even trendy clothes—you're effectively **losing money.** These items either lose their value quickly or **don't generate any income.**

Self-made millionaires, on the other hand, focus their money on **building wealth through ownership.** Instead of spending on liabilities, they invest in assets—things that appreciate in value or provide ongoing income.

What is Ownership?

Ownership is the state or status of having something of inherent value and the capacity to create wealth in the long run. Great examples are real estate investments, equities, businesses, or even concepts like books or patents.

Why is ownership important?

- **Appreciation:** Assets like real estate, stocks, and businesses tend to appreciate over time, increasing your wealth.
- **Cash Flow:** Many assets generate **passive income**—money that flows in regularly, whether you're actively working or not.
- **Control:** When you own something, you control it. You decide when and how to sell or generate income from it.

Owning assets gives you the **freedom** to build wealth without being tied to a job or working long hours. In fact, **the more assets you own,** the closer you are to financial freedom.

The Difference Between Assets and Liabilities

Let's take a moment to talk about the difference between **assets** and **liabilities**—two key concepts that self-made millionaires understand well.

- **Assets** are things that **put money in your pocket.** They appreciate over time or generate passive income. Examples include rental properties, stocks, businesses, intellectual property, etc.
- **Liabilities**, on the other hand, are things that **take money out of your pocket.** They depreciate over time or incur ongoing costs. Examples are expensive clothing, credit card debt, and cars.

The Millionaire Mindset:

Self-made millionaires focus on acquiring **assets** while minimizing or eliminating **liabilities**. It is understood, the more assets that are owned, the more wealth can be accumulated. They invest their money in ways that make their money **work for them**—instead of the other way around.

How to Invest When You're Not Rich

Most likely the greatest myth is the belief that you need to be rich to invest. But that couldn't be further from the truth. You don't need to have millions of dollars to start building wealth through ownership. Here are a few practical steps to start investing even if you don't think you're "rich" yet:

1. **Start Small:** You don't have to buy a mansion or a fleet of rental properties to start. Begin with **small investments** like stocks, bonds, or even investing in a business or side hustle.
2. **Use Your Time:** Even if you don't have a lot of money, you have time. Start investing time in learning how to invest, it can be taking a course on stock trading or studying the real estate market.
3. **Leverage Others' Money:** One powerful way to get started in real estate, for example, is by **using other people's money** (OPM). You can invest in real estate through syndications, partnerships, or other forms of joint ventures that allow you to get started with little or no money down.

Automate Your Investments: Set up automatic investments to build your portfolio gradually. Investing is easier than ever, with just a few clicks you can set up recurring investments in ETFs or index funds.

The Power of Cash Flow Over Net Worth

Most people focus on building their **net worth**—the total value of their assets minus liabilities. But here's a secret that most people don't realize: **Cash flow is more important than net worth.**

Net worth is a static figure. It's the sum of your assets on paper. However, **cash flow** is the money that comes into your pocket regularly, providing you with the freedom to live your life without worrying about running out of money.

One **would ask, why is cash flow so important?**

One of the reasons is cash flow gives you the freedom to have options. With consistent, reliable income generated by assets like rental properties, stocks, or businesses, you don't have to rely on a 9-to-5 job to pay the bills anymore. Also, cash flow allows you the opportunity to invest, reinvest, and build wealth at a much faster pace.

Easy Ways to Start Investing Without Being Rich First

You don't need a fortune to start investing, but you do need a strategy. Here are a few simple ways to start building your investment portfolio:

1. **Invest in Index Funds:** Index funds are one of the easiest ways to invest in the stock market without taking on excessive risk. They allow you to own a **broad market of stocks** with just a small initial investment.
2. **Start Real Estate Investing with REITs: Real Estate Investment Trusts** (REITs) allow you to invest in real estate without buying property. You can start with as little as $500 and still gain exposure to the real estate market.
3. **Crowdfunding Platforms:** There are several platforms that allow you to invest in **startups** or **real estate projects** with small amounts of money. Sites like Fundrise or Crowdstreet let you begin investing with $500 or less.
4. **Peer-to-Peer Lending:** Peer-to-peer lending platforms let you invest in personal loans to individuals or small businesses. As an investor, you earn a portion of the interest on the loans you fund.

Practical Wealth Tactics: Becoming an Investor, Not Just a Consumer

1 Conduct a "Consumer vs. Investor" Audit

- List your last 10 purchases—did they appreciate or depreciate in value?
- You can make a conscious effort to spend more on assets than liabilities.

2 Start Investing With Small Amounts

- Open a brokerage account and invest in index funds.
- Set up automatic transfers to an investment account.

3 Understand Cash Flow Investing

- Study real estate, dividend stocks, or business investments.
- Look for income-generating assets instead of speculative ones.

Key Takeaways

- Wealth comes from ownership, not just earning. Shift from being a **consumer to an investor.** As you shift from consumer to investor you will understand this is key for achieving financial freedom.

- **Ownership of assets** is the true path to wealth; these assets generate ongoing income and appreciate over time. **Assets** put money in your pocket, while **liabilities** take money out.

- Focus on **assets that generate income**, not just appreciate in value. Small, consistent investments grow exponentially over time.

- **Start investing small,** and use strategies like automation, leveraging others' money, and choosing **cash-flowing assets**. Do know that cash flow is more important than net worth as it provides financial freedom and the ability to reinvest.

Now that you've made it this far in your reading, and if you're taking action as you learn, you should be excited about the possibilities that come with owning assets. It's not about having a lot of money to start—it's about **changing your mindset** to prioritize **investing** over **spending**, and taking small but significant steps toward creating lasting wealth.

Reflection Exercise

What's one small step you can take today to start your journey as an investor?

Chapter 4

The Automation Shift

Make Money Work for You

(Not the Other Way Around)

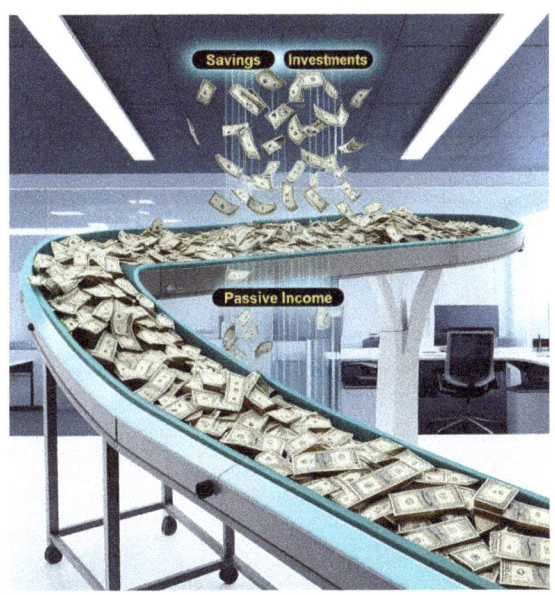

Jordan was terrible at saving money—until he set up automatic transfers. Every paycheck, a small portion went directly into investments **before he could even touch it.** Within five years, he had over $50,000 saved without effort. The secret? **Automation removes willpower from the equation** and makes wealth-building inevitable.

Chapter 4: The Automation Shift
Make Money Work for You
(Not the Other Way Around)

Introduction to the Automation Shift

In our fast-paced world, time is often our most valuable asset. The Automation Shift is about **making your money work for you**, rather than constantly working for money. It's about setting up systems that allow wealth-building to happen with minimal effort and intervention on your part.

Millionaires build wealth without sacrificing their time, energy, or sanity by utilizing automation. They've mastered the art of **automating financial processes**—from saving and investing to managing cash flow and wealth-building strategies.

In this chapter, you'll learn how to harness the power of **automation** in your financial life and how it can accelerate your journey to financial freedom.

The Problem with Manual Financial Management

If you're managing your finances manually, there's a good chance you're missing out on significant opportunities to grow your wealth.

This is because **manual management** of finances can be time-consuming, error-prone, and inefficient. If you're constantly moving money around, manually tracking investments, or worrying about every penny, you'll burn out long before you reach financial freedom.

The Solution: Automation.

I'm sure you can guess, self-made millionaires leverage systems to automate savings, investments, and financial processes. They don't manually track every expense or micromanage every transaction. Instead, they've set up systems that **work for them automatically**.

By automating certain aspects of your financial life, you can create **consistent wealth-building habits** without the constant effort or mental strain.

Why Automation Works

The key to building wealth is **compounding**—earning interest on interest, returns on returns. Automation is crucial because it allows you to **set the compounding process on autopilot**. It also removes the friction that can prevent you from consistently saving, investing, and growing your wealth.

Consider this:

When you set up automatic investments into a retirement fund, index fund, or real estate portfolio, your money starts working for you **immediately**—without your intervention. You don't have to think about it, track it, or worry about it. Every month, like clockwork, your investments grow and compound.

As you automate everything from savings to investments, you will began to accumulate wealth with less effort and greater predictability. It's this consistency that millionaires and billionaires use to build wealth.

The "Pay Yourself First" Strategy

One of the most powerful ways to automate your wealth-building process is by **"paying yourself first."** This strategy ensures that before any bills are paid or expenses are covered, a portion of your income goes into your savings or investments.

Wondering why this strategy is so effective?

1. **You prioritize your wealth-building:** By automating this process, you ensure that wealth-building comes first—before lifestyle inflation or unnecessary spending kicks in.
2. **You avoid the temptation to spend**: When the money is automatically deducted from your account and invested, you won't be tempted to overspend.
3. **You let the system do the work:** Your savings and investments will grow automatically, without you needing to lift a finger.

The result: **Automated wealth growth**, which doesn't require active participation, but instead happens steadily, month after month, year after year.

How to Establish Your Automated Wealth System

Now that we understand why automation is crucial, let's proceed into how to establish your automated wealth-building system.

1. **Automate Your Savings:**
    - Set up an automatic transfer from your checking account to a high-yield savings account or an emergency fund.
    - Set a specific percentage of your income to be transferred every month—whether it's 10%, 15%, or more. Consistency is the key.
2. **Automate Your Investments:**
    - Use platforms like **Robo-advisors** (e.g., Betterment, Wealthfront) to automatically invest your savings into diversified portfolios.
    - Set up automatic investments into **index funds** or **ETFs**. These are funds that often require little to no effort and are designed to grow over a period of time.
3. **Automate Your Bill Payments:**
    - Set up **automatic bill payments** for utilities, rent/mortgage, insurance, and credit card bills to ensure you're never late and avoid unnecessary fees.
4. **Automate Contributions to Retirement Accounts:**
    - Set up automatic contributions to your **401(k)**, **IRA**, or other retirement accounts. Automating retirement savings ensures that you don't have to think about it, and you can take full advantage of **compound interest** and **tax benefits**.
5. **Automate Debt Repayment:**
    - If you have debt, consider automating your monthly payments so you never miss a due date and can avoid late fees and interest hikes.

Consistency is super important in Automation

I know you've heard that Consistency is the key over and over again. Look at this way: consistency is the backbone of financial automation. The best part of automating your financial processes is that once they are set up, they run on their own, allowing you to focus on **other important aspects of your life.**

But consistency also means that **small, incremental investments** can snowball over time. By sticking to your automated system, you will start to see **significant wealth growth**, even with modest contributions.

The beauty of automation lies in its ability to create **momentum.** Just as the small snowball begins to grow as it rolls downhill, small investments can snowball into massive wealth over time, due to **compound interest.**

The Power of Time and Compounding

Let's talk about time—the most valuable asset you have.

Self-made millionaires don't focus on getting rich quickly. Instead, they understand the importance of **patience**. By automating their investments and letting their wealth grow over time, they create **financial snowballs** that compound faster than they could have ever anticipated.

For example, let's say you start investing $500 per month into an **index fund** that returns an average of 8% per year. After 30 years, you'll have invested a total of $180,000, but the **value of that investment could exceed $1.2 million** due to the power of compound interest.

The key to this growth? **Automation.** By setting it up once and letting time and compounding do the rest, you build wealth **without having to think about it constantly.**

Practical Wealth Tactics: Automating Your Wealth

1 Set Up Automatic Savings & Investments

- Automate a percentage of your income to go into savings and investments.
- Using apps like Acorns or Betterment can make investing effortless.

2 Leverage Business & Income Automation

- Create passive income through online businesses, print-on-demand, or affiliate marketing.
- Automate your freelance work by using outsourcing and digital tools.

3 Streamline Financial Management

- Use software like Mint or YNAB to track spending and investments.
- Set up auto-payments for bills to avoid late fees.

Key Takeaways

- **Automation** is the key to building wealth with minimal effort. Leverage technology to remove friction from making and managing money. By having automation systems in place you can create a system that works for you.

- **Pay yourself first:** Prioritize savings and investments before any other expenses. **Small contributions**, automated actions lead to big financial growth over time, especially with the power of **compound interest.**

- **Automate everything:** Savings, investments, bill payments, retirement contributions, and debt repayment. By fully automating, you free yourself from needing to constantly manage your money, so you can focus on other ways of growing your wealth and **enjoying life with more freedom.**

The Automation Shift is all about freeing up your time and mental energy while your wealth grows steadily and predictably. It's one of the most effective tools in your arsenal for reaching financial independence and securing long-term wealth.

Reflection Exercise

- What's one financial process you can automate today?

Chapter 5

The Frictionless Income Shift

Creating Multiple Income Streams

Aisha was exhausted from her job, trading time for money. She started selling digital planners online as a side project. At first, it made just $50 a month, but within a year, she was earning more than her salary **without extra effort**. She realized that **millionaires don't just work for money—they create money that works for them.**

Chapter 5: The Frictionless Income Shift

Creating Multiple Income Streams

Introduction to the Frictionless Income Shift

If you're working hard for a single paycheck, you're already doing what most people do. But self-made millionaires have figured out a better way: **they don't rely on just one income source.**

Instead, they create **multiple income streams** that work for them, often without requiring them to actively trade time for money. This is the principle to achieve financial freedom—and one of the key reasons why wealthy individuals continue to build their wealth even while they sleep.

In this chapter, we'll explore how to **diversify your income**, reduce reliance on a single paycheck, and create financial stability that's **as frictionless as possible.**

The "One Income = Risky" Principle

Self-made millionaires understand a crucial fact: **relying on a single income stream is risky**. If you lose your job, experience a pay cut, or your business suffers a downturn, your financial life could be in jeopardy.

Millionaires typically don't have **just one** source of income; they have several, often from different industries and sources, that continue to build wealth even if one stream temporarily dries up. This is why they prioritize creating multiple streams of income.

The Wealth Hack:

Even if you currently have one income stream, your goal should be to build **diversity**—to set up multiple sources of income that require little to no active involvement after the initial setup.

The Power of Passive & Semi-Passive Income

Let's break down two major types of income that millionaires use to multiply their wealth: **passive income** and **semi-passive income**.

Passive Income:

Passive income is money that you earn regularly without having to put in a constant amount of effort. This could include income from rental properties, dividends from investments, or royalties from books or intellectual property. Once you set it up, it's like a money machine that keeps running without constant attention.

Semi-Passive Income:

Semi-passive income requires some active involvement initially but eventually runs on its own. Think of businesses that require minimal day-to-day management, such as **e-commerce stores** (like dropshipping) or **digital products** (e-books, courses, etc.).

By combining both passive and semi-passive income streams, you create a financial ecosystem that **works for you automatically** while you focus on other areas of your life or business.

Simple Ways to Add Passive Income Streams

Starting with passive income may sound difficult, but there are easy ways to build these streams. The key is to **think long-term**, start small, and let your efforts compound over time.

These are some examples of how you can get started:

1. **Invest in Dividend Stocks:** The stock market offers many opportunities for passive income through **dividends.** By investing in companies that pay regular dividends, you create a reliable income stream that can grow over time with minimal maintenance.
2. **Real Estate Investments:** You don't have to own a large portfolio to generate passive income. Even starting with **a single rental property** can provide a steady stream of income. Platforms like **Airbnb** allow for semi-passive real estate income, where you can rent out property with minimal ongoing effort.
3. **Peer-to-Peer Lending:** Platforms like **LendingClub** allow you to lend money to individuals or small businesses and receive interest payments over time. This is a relatively simple way to generate passive income if you're willing to take on some risk.
4. **Create Digital Products:** E-books, online courses, and digital guides are perfect examples of products that can generate royalties and **revenue long after the work is done.** Once created, these products can be sold again and again, creating passive income.

Building Your Semi-Passive Income Streams

In addition to passive income, self-made millionaires often focus on **semi-passive income**, which offers a balance of initial work and long-term reward.

Here are a few strategies to set up semi-passive income:
1. **E-commerce & Dropshipping**: You don't need to manage inventory or even ship products yourself. With **dropshipping**, you can create an online store that sells products from suppliers who handle the fulfillment. Once the store is set up, you can generate income with little ongoing effort.
2. **Affiliate Marketing:** With affiliate marketing, you promote other people's products and earn commissions for every sale made through your referral link. **Creating a blog, YouTube channel, or website** that attracts traffic can provide a steady stream of income without needing to create your own products.
3. **Create and Sell Courses:** If you have expertise in a particular area, creating an **online course** is one of the best ways to generate semi-passive income. Platforms like **Udemy** and **Teachable** make it easy to create and sell courses to a global audience.
4. **Automated Online Businesses:** Set up **businesses that run on autopilot**—such as dropshipping stores or print-on-demand businesses—that require minimal active involvement once established.

Scaling Your Income Streams

Once you've created one or two passive or semi-passive income streams, the next step is to **scale** them. Scaling involves increasing the reach, volume, or impact of your income streams to generate more wealth with minimal extra effort.

Here's how to scale effectively:

1. **Outsource Tasks:** Many successful business owners outsource or hire others to handle the day-to-day operations. For example, if you have an e-commerce store, you can hire a **virtual assistant** to manage customer service or marketing. Outsourcing is a way for you to free up your time to focus on scaling your income streams.
2. **Leverage Technology:** Automation tools and software can help streamline business processes, such as **marketing, inventory management**, and **customer service,** allowing you to scale faster with less involvement.
3. **Reinvest Profits:** As your passive and semi-passive income streams start generating money, reinvest some of those profits into **new income streams** or into scaling existing ones. This will increase your wealth long-term.

Why Millionaires Love Scalable Businesses

One of the reasons millionaires focus on **scalable businesses** is that they allow for exponential growth. Scalable businesses can create a snowball effect through your efforts and investments. As your business grows, your income increases, often without much extra work from you.

Self-made millionaires typically love businesses that **don't require them to trade time for money.** The more systems they can automate, the more **they can multiply their income without sacrificing their time.**

Practical Wealth Tactics: Creating Multiple Streams of Income

Building multiple income streams doesn't have to be overwhelming—start small and scale up. Here's how:

1 Assess Your Current Income Streams
- Write down where your money currently comes from.
- Identify gaps—are you 100% reliant on a paycheck?

2 Choose One New Stream to Develop
- Side Hustle: Freelancing, consulting, or selling digital products.
- Passive Income: Investing in dividend stocks, rental properties, or creating online courses.
- Scalable Business: E-commerce, memberships, or affiliate marketing.

3 Set Up an Automated System
- Use tools like Zapier, Shopify, or ConvertKit to reduce manual work.
- Be sure to focus on businesses that don't require daily attention to generate income.

4 Reinvest Profits Into More Income Streams
- Take profits from one stream and invest them into another (e.g., use freelance income to buy dividend stocks).
- Scale by hiring, outsourcing, or automating tasks.

Key Takeaways

- Relying on one income source is risky—build diversify in your finances. **Multiple income streams** are crucial for financial freedom.
- Start with one additional stream and expand over time. **Passive and semi-passive income streams** are key to wealth building. You can start with simple strategies such as investing in stocks, real estate, or creating digital products.
- Automation is key to reducing effort while increasing income. **Scaling your income streams** through outsourcing, technology, and reinvesting profits is essential for long-term growth.
- The wealthiest people reinvest earnings into multiple assets. **Millionaires love scalable businesses** because they allow them to grow their wealth exponentially with minimal effort.

The **Frictionless Income Shift** is about working smarter, not harder. By setting up income streams that require little to no active participation, you can build a stable and growing income that doesn't demand your full-time attention.

Reflection Exercise

What's one new income stream you can start today? What's the first step?

Chapter 6

The Network Shift

Who You Spend Time With Determines Your Wealth

David struggled for years to build his business—until he started networking with people who were **already successful.** One introduction led to a mentor, then to an investor, and suddenly, his company took off. Lesson? **Your network isn't just who you know—it's who can help you grow.**

Chapter 6: The Network Shift
Who You Spend Time With Determines Your Wealth

Introduction to the Network Shift

When it comes to wealth-building, your network is one of your most powerful assets. The people you surround yourself with—whether personally or professionally—shape your thoughts, actions, and opportunities. This principle is known as "**Your network = your net worth.**"

Self-made millionaires understand that surrounding themselves with the **right people** can accelerate their wealth-building journey. They don't just network to socialize; they network strategically to **expand their influence, opportunities, and resources.**

In this chapter, we'll explore how **who you spend time with** directly impacts your wealth and how to strategically build a network that aligns with your financial goals.

The "Success Circle Formula"

To become wealthy, you need to surround yourself with people who will **elevate you,** challenge you, and inspire you to grow. This is known as your "Success Circle".

The Success Circle Formula works like this:

- **5% of the people in your circle should be ahead of you financially,** inspiring you to level up.
- **20% should be at your level,** helping you stay grounded and motivated.
- **75% should be people you can help or mentor,** because teaching others reinforces your own knowledge and keeps you sharp.

With this formula, you to can continue to learn from those who are ahead of you, build quality relationships with peers, and pay it forward by giving back to guide or assist others. It's about creating **symbiotic relationships** that nurture both personal and financial growth.

Why Self-Made Millionaires Prioritize Their Network

One of the biggest reasons **self-made millionaires** are so successful is their **ability to leverage the knowledge and resources of others.** They understand that their wealth isn't solely dependent on their individual efforts but on their **connections** and **relationships** with other high achievers.

Millionaires intentionally build **high-value relationships** with individuals who can help them **achieve their financial goals**, such as business partners, mentors, investors, and like-minded peers. Intriguingly, they don't just hang out with people—they cultivate relationships that provide value in both directions.

Here's why the network is crucial:

- **Access to opportunities:** The right connections can introduce you to opportunities you might never have encountered on your own.
- **Mentorship:** Learning from someone who has already walked the path you want to follow can save you years of mistakes.
- **Knowledge sharing**: Millionaires frequently exchange insights, strategies, and best practices, which keeps them ahead of the curve.
- **Increased influence:** As your network grows, so does your influence. The more people you know, the more resources and opportunities come your way.

How to Find the Right People

Building a wealth-building network requires **intentionality**. Here are a few tips for finding and attracting the right people into your circle:

1. **Attend Industry Events and Conferences:** Get involved in events where **successful people in your field** gather. Most of the time, they are a goldmine to identify people who have your type of thinking and people who can provide their knowledge, experience, and even collaborations.
2. **Join Mastermind Groups:** Mastermind groups are an ideal way to be surrounded by driven individuals. These groups are productive as they bring like-minded people together with the goal of sharing knowledge, brainstorming solutions, and helping one another achieve their goals.
3. **Be Active on Social Media:** Platforms like **LinkedIn, Twitter, and Instagram** allow you to engage with influencers, thought leaders, and other wealthy individuals. Mainly, through offering valuable content, communication, and sharing worth, you can begin creating beneficial relationships on the internet.
4. **Get Involved in Local Business or Community Groups:** Whether it's your local Chamber of Commerce or an entrepreneurial meetup, these groups are great places to meet people who are building wealth locally. **Volunteer, take leadership roles,** and **get involved** to build your presence and connections.
5. **Work with a Mentor or Coach:** A mentor who has achieved the success you're aspiring to can guide you and introduce you to a network of other high-level professionals. Don't just seek advice; ask for introductions to key people in their network.

Building Relationships That Create Value

Building a **network** isn't just about getting to know people for what they can do for you. True wealth-building networks are **based on value exchange.** Here's how to foster meaningful relationships:

1. **Offer Help First:** Before you ask for something, offer something. Whether it's an introduction to someone in your network, sharing valuable information, or helping them solve a problem, providing value first is the best way to establish trust and create reciprocity.
2. **Show Genuine Interest:** Millionaires don't network just to get ahead—they genuinely take an interest in people and their successes. It is good to ask questions, listen carefully, and show empathy. Building meaningful connections will open doors for you in ways surface-level interactions will not.
3. **Be Consistent:** Networking isn't a one-time thing. Keep in touch with people over time, even when you don't need anything. Send an occasional check-in email, message, or offer to grab coffee. Stay **visible** and **relevant** in your network, and the opportunities will follow.
4. **Build a Personal Brand:** To attract high-quality people, you must be **clear about who you are and what you offer.** Building a personal brand around your expertise and value proposition will make you magnetic to others who want to connect with you.

How to Use Your Network to Accelerate Your Wealth

Your network doesn't just provide advice or emotional support—it can be a **direct catalyst** for your wealth-building success. Here's how to leverage it:

1. **Partner Up for Business Ventures:** Often, the best way to build wealth is through collaborations. Network to team up with others who have complementary skills or resources, as they can help you to scale your business faster and reach a larger audience.
2. **Get Introduced to Investors:** Your network is a goldmine for finding potential investors who believe in your vision. You can pitch your business idea, receive mentorship, and secure the capital you need to expand through your connections.
3. **Learn from the Best:** Your network is filled with people who've already walked the path you want to follow. The best part, networks help you learn from others' successes and failures, gain insights to help you avoid common pitfalls, and **shorten your learning curve.**
4. **Create Accountability:** Surrounding yourself with ambitious, driven people who hold you accountable will push you to work harder and smarter. Mentors, peers, and advisors who check in on your progress are good to have as it keeps you moving forward.

The Power of Mentorship

Mentorship is one of the **most powerful tools** in the millionaire's toolkit. Having someone to guide you through the intricacies of wealth-building can dramatically shorten the time it takes to reach your goals.

Finding the right mentor means looking for someone who's been successful in the areas you want to succeed in. Ideally, they should be someone who has **already navigated the path** and can help you avoid costly mistakes.

Practical Wealth Tactics: Leveling Up Your Success Circle

1 Audit Your Current Network

- List the five people you spend the most time with. Are they financially motivated?
- You should ask yourself, do they inspire or drain you?

2 Find and Connect With Growth-Minded People

- Join masterminds, online communities, and local business groups.
- Build genuine relationships by engaging in high-value conversations and offering help to others.

3 Seek Out Mentors and Coaches

- Identify someone who has achieved the financial goals you want.
- Offer value first—ask for advice without expecting handouts.

4 Create a Networking Strategy

- Attend at least one event per quarter where high achievers gather.
- Use social media platforms like, LinkedIn, Twitter, or local meetups to engage with potential mentors.

Key Takeaways

- **Your network = your net worth.** Surround yourself with winners; people who will inspire, challenge, and elevate you to new levels of success.

- Actively engage in growth-minded communities. **The Success Circle Formula** is essential for wealth-building: 5% ahead of you, 20% at your level, 75% you can mentor.

- Build genuine relationships, not just transactional connections. **Strategically build relationships** by offering value first, showing interest, and staying consistent.

- **Leverage your network** to partner up for business ventures, get introduced to investors, and learn from those who've already achieved what you want.

- Seek out mentors who have already achieved your desired success. **Mentorship** is critical for fast-tracking your success—find a mentor who can guide you on your wealth-building journey.

The **Network Shift** is about strategically curating your circle to create **opportunities for wealth** and success. It's not about the number of people you know but about the **quality** of those relationships. Your network, if carefully cultivated, will become one of your most powerful wealth-building assets.

Reflection Exercise

Who is one person you can reach out to today that could elevate your financial journey?

Chapter 7

The Legacy Shift

Build Generational Wealth

& Financial Freedom

As a child, **Sophia** watched her grandfather build a business from scratch. But what amazed her most wasn't how he made money—it was how he **taught the family to manage, invest, and pass it down.** Today, generations later, his legacy still thrives. The lesson? **True wealth isn't just about you—it's about what you leave behind.**

Chapter 7: The Legacy Shift

Build Generational Wealth & Financial Freedom

Introduction to the Legacy Shift

By the time you reach this chapter, you have already made significant strides in changing your mindset, mastering high-income skills, investing wisely, and building powerful networks. But there's one more shift that takes everything to the next level: **The Legacy Shift.**

This shift is about more than just accumulating wealth—it's about creating a **legacy** that lasts beyond your lifetime. It's about leaving **a blueprint for future generations** to follow, ensuring that your wealth continues to grow long after you're gone.

Self-made millionaires understand that true wealth isn't measured by what they can spend today, but by what they can pass on tomorrow. In this chapter, you'll learn how to build **generational wealth**, preserve your hard-earned financial success, and create a legacy that will last for generations.

The Concept of Generational Wealth

Generational wealth is the wealth that **passes down** from one generation to the next, ensuring that your children, grandchildren, and even great-grandchildren have the financial freedom and resources to thrive. The goal is to **break the cycle** of living paycheck to paycheck and build wealth that can support multiple generations.

Unlike traditional wealth, which is often consumed during a person's lifetime, generational wealth is **strategically built, protected, and passed down** to create **lasting financial stability** for future generations. By focusing on the long-term, you can create a **legacy of financial security** that outlives your own lifetime.

The "Freedom Number" – What You Need to Retire

A crucial part of the legacy shift is understanding your **"Freedom Number"**—the amount of money you need to retire comfortably without worrying about running out of funds. It's the **number** that represents the financial independence you've always dreamed of.

To calculate your **Freedom Number**, consider the following:

- **Monthly Expenses:** How much do you spend each month to maintain your current lifestyle?

- **Desired Retirement Age:** When do you want to retire, and how many years until then?

- **Expected Rate of Return:** How much growth do you expect from your investments?

- **Longevity:** How long do you want to ensure that you're financially secure in retirement?

Your **Freedom Number** is essentially your roadmap to financial independence. It tells you how much you need to save and invest in order to live off your wealth without needing to actively work.

The Psychology of Long-Term Thinking

Most people's financial decisions are based on **short-term thinking**—the "quick fix" mentality that leads to making decisions that seem right in the moment but cause problems in the long run. This is where the wealthy **differ** from the average person.

Self-made millionaires have learned to adopt a **long-term mindset**. They think decades ahead, not days or months. They understand that wealth-building is a marathon, not a sprint, and that real success requires the patience to wait for the **compound effect** to work its magic.

The psychology of **long-term thinking** is about **delayed gratification** and trusting that the sacrifices you make today will lead to **abundant rewards** in the future. Millionaires consistently make decisions that benefit them in the long term, not just in the present moment.

Strategies for Building Generational Wealth

To truly build generational wealth, you need a plan that goes beyond just saving money. Here are several strategies used by the wealthy to ensure that their wealth continues to grow long after they're gone:

1. **Investing in Assets, Not Liabilities:** Millionaires focus on **building assets**—things that grow in value, like real estate, stocks, and businesses. They avoid liabilities that drain resources, such as cars, credit card debt, and other depreciating assets.
2. **Life Insurance & Trusts:** Using tools like **life insurance** and **trusts** is a common strategy to ensure wealth is passed down efficiently and without heavy tax burdens. Life insurance can provide liquidity, while trusts can help manage and protect wealth for future generations.
3. **Investing in Real Estate:** Real estate is a proven method for building long-term wealth. Millionaires often use real estate to build **passive income** and create a **portfolio of appreciating assets** that generate wealth over time.
4. **Teach Financial Literacy to the Next Generation:** The wealthiest families know that to **preserve wealth**, you must **teach your children** how to manage money properly. This includes instilling the value of hard work, saving, investing, and making wise financial decisions.
5. **Create a Family Business or Investment Portfolio:** Building a business or a portfolio of investments that can be passed down is a powerful way to create a **legacy**. Whether it's a family business or an investment strategy, these assets can continue to grow and support future generations.

The Importance of Patience and Preservation

Building generational wealth isn't just about accumulating assets—it's also about **preserving** them. Millionaires know that the most important part of wealth-building is to avoid **making hasty decisions** that could jeopardize long-term financial security.

Here are some key principles of wealth **preservation:**

- **Avoid speculative investments:** Millionaires typically stay away from risky investments that could wipe out wealth.

- **Diversification:** A diverse portfolio helps spread out risk and ensures that one bad investment won't destroy wealth.

- **Maintain a long-term vision:** Wealth is often lost because people chase **short-term gains**. Focus on growing your assets steadily over time.

Making Your Wealth Work for the Next Generation

When building a legacy, it's essential that your wealth not only benefits you but that it continues to work for future generations. The goal is to set up systems that ensure your wealth grows and remains secure:

Create a Legacy Fund: This is a pool of money or assets dedicated to future generations. A legacy fund can be used for educational expenses, starting businesses, or as a safety net.

Teach Generational Wealth: Use every opportunity to **teach your children** or heirs about how to manage wealth responsibly. This involves setting up **family financial meetings** and involving younger generations in discussions about long-term planning.

Legacy Investments: Focus on investments that have the potential to grow for many years, such as real estate, blue-chip stocks, or long-term bonds.

Practical Wealth Tactics: Building Generational Wealth

1 Define Your "Freedom Number"

- Calculate how much passive income you need to cover expenses.
- Reverse-engineer a long-term plan to get there.

2 Document Your Wealth Plan

- Write down your investment, estate planning, and asset distribution goals.
- Consider trusts, wills, and tax-efficient wealth transfer.

3 Teach Financial Literacy to Your Family

- Share wealth-building lessons with your children or loved ones.
- Involve family members in investing, budgeting, and asset management.

4 Scale Beyond Yourself

- Consider philanthropy, endowments, or creating a family investment fund.
- Focus on impact—wealth isn't just about money, but what you do with it.

Key Takeaways

- Wealth isn't just about you—it's about **leaving a lasting impact. Generational wealth** is about passing down financial resources that can support future generations.

- Set a clear financial target for **freedom and security**. Calculate your **"Freedom Number"** to determine exactly what you need to retire and achieve financial independence.

- Adopt a **long-term mindset**, focusing on **delayed gratification** and making decisions that benefit your future, not just your present.

- Use strategies like **investing in assets, life insurance,** and **trusts** to build and preserve wealth.

- Surely, educate future generations about financial literacy and the importance of making wise money decisions. Teaching financial literacy ensures wealth lasts **for generations.**

- **Patience and preservation** are essential components of building lasting wealth. Think beyond yourself—create a **legacy of abundance.**

The Legacy Shift is about building wealth that not only supports you but also supports your children, grandchildren, and beyond. When you adopt this shift, you're no longer just working for your own success but ensuring that the next generation has the tools and resources to continue what you've started. This is how you leave a lasting **legacy of financial freedom.**

Reflection Exercise

What is one step you can take today to ensure your wealth outlives you?

Conclusion

Your 7-Shift Game Plan

A Quick-Action Plan to Apply

All 7 Shifts in Real Life

Conclusion: Your 7-Shift Game Plan

A Quick-Action Plan to Apply All 7 Shifts in Real Life

Congratulations on Completing Your 7 Shifts!

You've reached the end of **The Wealth Hack: 7 Simple Shifts to Go from Broke to Financially Free**.

Congratulations on making it this far! By now, you've discovered the power of shifting your mindset, embracing high-income skills, focusing on investments, and building the kind of legacy that lasts for generations.

But here's the thing: knowing about these shifts isn't enough. **Implementation** is the key. Now it's time to take action and integrate these 7 shifts into your daily life. It's not just about reading this book—it's about **transforming your financial future** by applying what you've learned.

So, let's get to it. Below is your **quick-action game plan** to begin applying the 7 shifts and changing your financial life.

Shift #1 – The Millionaire Mindset Shift

The first step to changing your financial future is adopting the **Millionaire Mindset**. This means:

1. **Reprogram your money beliefs:** Replace the limiting beliefs of scarcity with the empowering belief in abundance.
2. **Overcome negative self-talk:** Learn to identify and challenge any thoughts that hold you back financially.
3. **Embrace your new identity**: See yourself as a person worthy of financial freedom and success.

Action Steps:

- Write down **three money beliefs** you want to shift from negative to positive.

- Create a daily **affirmation practice** to reinforce your new, abundant mindset.

Shift #2 – The High-Income Skill Shift

High-income skills are the key to building financial security and independence. **Stop trading time for money** and start trading value.

1. **Identify your core skills** and build on them.
2. **Master the art of skill-stacking**: Combine multiple high-income skills to become more valuable in the market.
3. **Commit to constant learning**: Wealthy people are never done learning. They consistently improve their skills and expand their value.

Action Steps:

- **List 3 high-income skills** you want to master and develop.

- **Create a learning schedule:** Dedicate at least 30 minutes a day to learning or practicing one of these skills.

Shift #3 – The Ownership Shift

Self-made millionaires understand that wealth comes from **owning assets,** not just earning income. Start focusing on building and acquiring assets that work for you.

1. **Shift from consumer to investor:** Focus on purchasing assets that generate passive income, such as stocks, real estate, or businesses.
2. **Understand the Cash Flow Over Net Worth Rule:** Prioritize cash flow from investments over just accumulating wealth for the sake of having a high net worth.
3. **Get started with small investments:** You don't need to be rich to begin investing. Start small, and let compound interest work its magic.

Action Steps:

- **Choose one investment** to start learning about (e.g., real estate, stocks, or mutual funds).

- **Set up an automatic investment plan** for monthly contributions to your chosen asset.

Shift #4 – The Automation Shift

One of the key habits of wealthy people is the ability to **automate** their finances. This means setting up systems that make saving, investing, and wealth-building easier and less time-consuming.

1. **Pay Yourself First:** Automate your savings and investments to ensure you prioritize your financial future.
2. **Set up automatic bill payments:** This eliminates the need to think about your bills each month, freeing up mental energy.
3. **Create a low-maintenance financial system** that works for you.

Action Steps:

- Set up **automatic transfers** to your savings or investment account on payday.

- Automate **bill payments** so you're not late on your expenses, which also improves your credit score.

Shift #5 – The Frictionless Income Shift

Wealthy people know that **one income is risky**, so they create multiple streams of income. This can be passive, semi-passive, or active income from different sources.

1. **Diversify your income streams**: Don't rely on just one source of income. Explore side businesses, freelance work, or investments that can create additional cash flow.
2. **Embrace passive income:** Look for opportunities where you can earn without constantly trading time for money (e.g., rental properties, dividend-paying stocks, or online businesses).
3. **Optimize your existing skills** to generate income in new ways.

Action Steps:

- **Identify one new income stream** you can start in the next 30 days.

- Research **one passive income source** (e.g., real estate, dividend stocks, or an online business) and create a plan to invest or build.

Shift #6 – The Network Shift

Your network determines your net worth. **Surrounding yourself with the right people** can open doors and provide valuable insights and opportunities.

1. **Build relationships with successful people:** Surround yourself with individuals who inspire you and challenge you to think bigger.
2. **Leverage mentorship:** Seek out mentors who have already achieved the financial success you desire.
3. **Make networking intentional:** Be strategic in who you spend your time with and look for ways to add value to others.

Action Steps:

- **Reach out to one person** in your network or industry who can help you grow your wealth.

- **Attend one networking event** or join an online community related to your financial goals.

Shift #7 – The Legacy Shift

The final shift is about building **generational wealth.** Wealth isn't just about what you can spend in your lifetime—it's about what you can leave behind.

1. **Build a financial plan** that considers long-term wealth and preservation.
2. **Teach your children financial literacy** so they can continue to grow and protect the wealth you've built.
3. **Set up a trust or legacy fund** to ensure your wealth is passed down with minimal tax implications.

Action Steps:

- **Calculate your Freedom Number** to see exactly how much you need to retire and live comfortably.

- **Start planning for generational wealth** by setting up a financial plan or trust.

A Challenge for You

It's time to take the next step. Over the next 30 days, commit to implementing **one action step** from each shift. These small changes, when compounded over time, will lead to big results.

Remember, the journey to financial freedom and wealth-building is a process. It requires **discipline, persistence**, and a willingness to **learn and grow.** The key is to **take consistent action** and stay focused on the long-term vision.

Resources & Next Steps

Here are a few resources to help you along your journey to financial freedom:

- **Books to read:** Expand your knowledge with titles like *Rich Dad Poor Dad*, *The Psychology of Money*, *Tools of Titans*, and *The Millionaire Next Door*.

- **Courses & programs:** Look into online courses that focus on personal finance, investing, or entrepreneurship.

- **Mentorship:** Seek out mentors who have already achieved the success you're after.

Stay committed to your goals, and don't be afraid to adjust your approach as you go. Financial freedom isn't just a dream—it's a result of the **7 shifts** that will change your life.

Bonus 1:

Wealth Tracking &

Goal-Setting Workbook

Bonus:

Wealth Tracking & Goal-Setting Workbook

Introduction to the Workbook

Congratulations once again on completing The Wealth Hack! Since you have learned about the 7 transformative shifts that will propel you toward financial freedom. It's time to now take action—and track your progress along the way.

This **Wealth Tracking & Goal-Setting Workbook** is designed to help you stay focused, measure your growth, and set actionable goals. By following this workbook, you'll gain clarity, create a path forward, and see tangible results as you apply the principles from *The Wealth Hack*.

Remember, tracking your progress isn't just about numbers; it's about **creating habits** that lead to financial success. **Stay committed** to tracking your journey and revisiting these goals regularly.

Part 1 – Define Your Financial Goals

Before you can track your wealth, you need to know where you're headed. The first step is **defining your financial goals.**

Action Steps:

1. Write down your **short-term financial goals** (6 months to 1 year).
   _____
   _____
   _____

2. Write down your **mid-term financial goals** (1 to 3 years).
   _____
   _____
   _____

3. Write down your **long-term financial goals** (3 years and beyond).
   _____
   _____
   _____

Questions to consider:

- What do you want your financial situation to look like in the next year, five years, and ten years?
   _____
   _____
   _____

- Do you want to pay off debt, save for retirement, or create multiple income streams?
   _____
   _____
   _____

Part 2 – Wealth Tracking

Now that you've set your goals, it's time to track your wealth-building progress. This part will guide you to measure your financial health in key areas.

Track the following monthly:

1. **Income Streams:** List your income sources (salary, investments, side businesses).
   _____
   _____

2. **Expenses:** Track your monthly expenses and identify areas for improvement.
   _____
   _____

3. **Savings:** Track how much you're saving each month and compare it to your set savings goal.
   _____
   _____

4. **Investments:** Monitor the growth or decline of your investments (stocks, real estate, mutual funds).
   _____
   _____

5. **Net Worth:** Keep a running total of your assets and liabilities to track your net worth over time.
   _____
   _____
   _____

Part 3 – Actionable Wealth Goals

Now let's turn these into specific, actionable steps. **Break down each goal into smaller actions** that you can implement each month. This will ensure that you don't get overwhelmed and make progress consistently.

Example:

- **Goal:** Build an emergency fund of $10,000 in one year.
    - **Action Steps:**
        - Save $833 each month for 12 months.
        - Automate a transfer of $833 to a separate savings account every payday.

- **Goal:**
  _____
  _____
  _____
  _____

    - **Action Steps:**
      _____
      _____
      _____
      _____

- **Goal:**
  _____
  _____
  _____
  _____

    - **Action Steps:**
      _____
      _____
      _____
      _____

Part 4 – Wealth Reflection and Adjustments

Every month, take a moment to reflect on your progress. What's working? What needs improvement? This reflection is a crucial part of staying on track.

Questions to ask yourself:

- Did you meet your savings and investment goals for the month?
  _____
  _____
  _____

- Which habits are helping you make progress?
  _____
  _____
  _____

- Where can you improve?
  _____
  _____
  _____

Bonus 2:

Resources &

Recommended Reading List

Resources & Recommended Reading List

Introduction to Resources & Recommended Reading

To continue on your journey toward financial freedom, it's important to **keep learning**. As I have referenced throughout this book, on the next page is a curated list of resources, books, and tools that will help you further develop your financial intelligence and implement the 7 shifts.

These recommendations will **expand your knowledge** in critical areas like wealth psychology, investing, entrepreneurship, and personal development. Be sure to take action with what you learn from these resources.

Recommended Books

1. **The Psychology of Money by Morgan Housel**
   - A deep dive into how emotions and biases impact financial decision-making. This book will enhance your understanding of the psychological factors behind wealth-building.

2. **Rich Dad Poor Dad by Robert Kiyosaki**
   - Learn the mindset shifts that distinguish the wealthy from the poor. Kiyosaki's teachings on financial literacy are foundational to understanding how to accumulate and grow wealth.

3. **Tools of Titans by Tim Ferriss**
   - A treasure trove of advice from some of the world's most successful entrepreneurs and high performers. This book covers a wide range of strategies for building wealth.

4. **The Millionaire Next Door by Thomas Stanley & William Danko**
   - A study of millionaires and how they live below their means, invest wisely, and build lasting wealth.

5. **Atomic Habits by James Clear**
   - A powerful guide to building small habits that compound into major success. This book is perfect for understanding how to create lasting wealth-building habits.

Podcasts & Online Courses

1. **The Dave Ramsey Show**
   - Learn practical advice on budgeting, debt management, and financial independence from one of the top financial experts in the world.

2. **BiggerPockets Podcast**
   - Perfect for those interested in real estate investing. BiggerPockets shares strategies, tips, and inspiring success stories from real estate investors.

3. **Rich Dad's Financial Education (Online Course)**
   - This course offers a deep dive into financial education, focusing on understanding money, investing, and building wealth through asset acquisition.

Tools & Financial Apps

1. **Mint**
   - A powerful budgeting and financial tracking tool that allows you to manage your finances, track expenses, and monitor your savings and investments.

2. **Personal Capital**
   - Helps you track your net worth and investments, providing an overview of your financial health and retirement planning.

3. **Acorns**
   - A simple app that rounds up your purchases and invests the difference into a diversified portfolio, helping you start investing with small amounts.

Acknowledgements

& Final Words

Thank You

Acknowledgments & Final Words

Acknowledgments

Writing The Wealth Hack: 7 Simple Shifts to Go from Broke to Financially Free has been an incredible journey. I want to extend my deepest gratitude to the following people and resources that helped make this book possible:

- **To my family and friends,** for their constant support and belief in my vision.

- **To the mentors and thought leaders** whose work inspired me to write this book: Robert Kiyosaki, Morgan Housel, Tim Ferriss, Thomas Stanley, and William Danko, among others.

- **To the countless individuals** who shared their personal stories of financial transformation, which served as the foundation for this work.

This book wouldn't have come to life without you all. Thank you for your guidance and encouragement.

Final Words

The journey to financial freedom is not a sprint; it's a marathon. You may face challenges along the way, but with **dedication, patience**, and the **7 shifts** you've learned, you can absolutely change your financial future.

Remember that **success is a series of small steps**, and the key to achieving your financial dreams is to stay committed, adapt, and learn from each experience.

Thank you for reading *The Wealth Hack,* and I wish you all the best as you embark on this exciting journey toward financial independence!

About the Author

C.C. Gayle is an entrepreneur and self-improvement enthusiast on a journey to unlock financial freedom. As someone who once faced the same financial struggles many people do, Gayle became obsessed with understanding how self-made millionaires think, make decisions, and create lasting wealth. This book is the result of that journey, blending science-backed wealth psychology, mindset shifts, and practical strategies into a simple, actionable roadmap.

Unlike traditional financial "gurus," Gayle isn't a financial expert but rather a real person applying these principles in everyday life—and sharing the insights along the way. Passion for personal growth, financial independence, and helping others make lasting changes is the driving force behind this work.

Outside of writing and exploring new wealth-building insights, Gayle finds joy in travel, quality time with family, and soaking up wisdom from today's most influential thought leaders.

Loved this book?

Help others start their journey to financial freedom.

✅ Share *The Wealth Hack* with a friend.

✅ Grab more copies at: www.ccgayle.com

Every copy supports the mission to empower everyday people with mindset and money tools that actually work.

Acknowledgments

First and foremost, **thank you**—yes, you!

Writing this book was a journey, but it wouldn't mean anything without **readers like you** who are committed to transforming their financial future. Your willingness to challenge old beliefs, embrace new strategies, and take action is what truly brings these pages to life.

To those who picked up this book with the hope of changing their financial story—**I see you.** Whether you're just starting out, struggling to break through, or already on your way to financial freedom, know that every shift you make, every step forward, is a victory.

A special thank you to everyone who has supported this book—family, friends, and the incredible minds whose work has shaped the insights within these pages. Your encouragement, feedback, and belief in this project kept me going.

Most importantly, if this book helps you in any way, I ask just one favor: **Pay it forward.** Share what you've learned, encourage someone else on their journey, and help create a world where financial freedom isn't just for the few, but for anyone willing to make the shift.

With gratitude,

CC Gayle

www.ingramcontent.com/pod-product-compliance
Lightning Source LLC
Chambersburg PA
CBHW040232110526
44582CB00001B/23